THE ART OF

Seduction

The Art of

RICHARD CRAZE

Seduction

 A GODSFIELD BOOK

Library of Congress Cataloging-in-Publication Data Available

Published in 1999 by Sterling Publishing Company, Inc.
387 Park Avenue South, New York, NY 10016

© 1999 Godsfield Press
Text © 1999 Richard Craze

Designed by
THE BRIDGEWATER BOOK COMPANY

Distributed in Canada by Sterling Publishing,
c/o Canadian Manda Group, One Atlantic Avenue
Suite 105, Toronto, Ontario, Canada M6K 3E7
Distributed in Australia by Capricorn Link (Australia) Pty Ltd
P.O. Box 6651, Baulkham Hills Business Centre, NSW 2153 Australia

Printed and bound in Hong Kong

ISBN 0-8069-7074-X

CONTENTS

Introduction

IN THE UNITED STATES recently a new syndrome was reported, which has become known as the "playboy syndrome." This is when one lover is unhappy with a partner because the partner fails to live up to some fictitious ideal they may have about physical beauty—an ideal they may have got from magazines such as *Playboy*—and this syndrome affects women just as much as men. Sex manuals perpetuate this fictitious ideal as well. This is not a sex manual.

The centerfolds in *Playboy* magazine aren't real—not in the sense that people look like that in real life. The photographs are airbrushed, the images are manipulated to a great extent by clever computer programs to make legs look longer, breasts larger, and skin more perfect. Sex manuals are manipulated by their writers to make it seem that if we're not enjoying total and climactic sex all the time we have somehow failed.

This book aims to offer suggestions and ideas about how you can enhance and improve your sexual excitement—mainly in seduction—by using what you've got. You don't need to learn any new or revolutionary sex techniques, nor do you need to change partners or lose twenty pounds in weight or buy any complicated or bizarre sex toys—all you've got to do is work with what you've got. We all have blemishes; we all fail sexually from time to time; we all suffer from low libido at some time; we all get tired and don't want to have wild passionate sex at the end of a long, busy working day; we all suffer from

children giving us no privacy or space; we all look a bit the worse for wear first thing in the morning. This book is for real people with real expectations; people who want to get a bit more out of their sex life without having to become sexual athletes or gymnasts; people who want to pep it up a bit and rekindle some of the lost passion they had when they first met.

This is a book about how to find again those thrilling moments of seductive encounters, how to put a bit of fun back into sex, and how to help sex maintain and improve a long-term relationship. In this day and age of AIDS, unwanted pregnancies, infectious diseases, alimony and divorce it makes sense to stay with the partner you've got. If you do swap your partner, you'll only end up back where you were, eventually. Working with what you've got might be a challenge but at least it's realistic—moving on whenever things go bad or fail to live up to your expectations is unrealistic and hurtful both to your lover and to you.

If you think you're going to find any tips on how to meet a woman or attract a new man into your life, forget it; this is a book for lovers who already love each other and just want to make that love more profound and deeper—for lovers who already know each other pretty well sexually and want to take that knowledge one step further.

You may think that seduction is all about the first time you get someone to take their clothes off and

make love with you—wrong. Seduction is about any time you get someone to take their clothes off and make love with you—even if they've done it thousands of times already. If you don't seduce your lover each and every time afresh, what are you doing with them? Assuming? Taking for granted? Ordering? Whatever you are doing, it isn't seduction. Seduction is treating people with respect and equality—just like you did when you first met them. We grow lazy and indifferent to our lover's needs over time and *The Art of Seduction* is about getting rid of that laziness and replacing the indifference with excitement, intrigue, passion, and arousal. This book will not tell you that you have to make love so many times a week, or achieve orgasm at least three times in each lovemaking session, or even that you should achieve it at all. What it sets out to do is encourage couples who are in a stable relationship to experiment with their sexuality,

arouse their passions, be honest with each other, be prepared to try some new things, and—most important—have some fun. Without fun, and laughter of course, sex is a deadly serious, and deadly dull, business. This book is here to help you lighten up and play around with each other.

It explores the senses one by one and suggests ways of improving what you do with them, and offers some new ideas for you to try. For instance, you might like to look at the *Touch* section: have you ever tried holding your lover's head in your hands and stroked their eyelids as they reach orgasm? Or how about seeing what sort of reaction you get from each of your lover's erogenous zones if you kiss them, tickle them, lick them, or suck them.

Look at the *Taste* section—here you might like to try making your own love potions—how many aphrodisiacs actually work anyway? You can even try your

8

hand at cooking rude food for your lover—cooking in the nude, of course.

The *Sound* section explores how you can use your ears to increase your sexual excitement. When did you last make love with Wagner? Or would you prefer all of the Rolling Stones? And how about practicing having an orgasm—make it the loudest you've ever had.

The *Sight* section is about turning your lover on with visual stimuli, as well as the art of lighting, makeup, and sexy underwear—for him and her.

In the *Smell* section you can explore the effects perfumes and aftershave have on lovers, as well as using flowers, herbs, and incense to create an erotic effect. The last section—*All the Senses*—explores the role libido plays in lovemaking and how, using massage, foreplay, and loveplay, you can improve and maintain your libido.

But first we need to look at seduction in a little more detail, so the book starts with two sections to take you through such things as *Setting the Scene* and the *Time and Place*. These will give you some ideas for improving your seduction techniques by a careful choice of timing, location, atmosphere, and suitability. It's all very well inviting your lover to make love on the kitchen table but if the children are still eating supper there, and the curtains aren't closed, and you have nosy neighbors, you can guarantee your wild night of sexy passion just isn't going to be the success you had hoped for! By careful planning and forethought, however, you can help your lover achieve pleasure as well as having some yourself.

So, send the children to bed early, close the curtains, clear the table, and go for it. Why not? Who knows, maybe you'll rediscover the old you, the younger, more seductive you, and that can't be a bad thing.

Nothing can be more off-putting to a lover than having ill-prepared sex. If your lover is worth making love to, then it is worth the effort of setting the scene properly.

Setting the Scene

SETTING THE SCENE means doing a little work beforehand. This is covered in detail further on in the book, but it is worth looking at it briefly here. For a start, you can prepare the room. Is it comfortable enough? Warm enough? No one likes taking off their clothes in a cold, uncomfortable environment.

For sudden unplanned seductions and lovemaking you would think that anywhere, any time was appropriate—but that's not the case. Even the most spontaneous bout of raunchy lovemaking is certainly improved and refined if a little work and effort has been done beforehand. You might like to think that you could just take your lover quickly and spontaneously on the kitchen table. But what if it is still covered with dirty plates and crockery? What if it simply isn't sturdy enough? What if the children have left a half-finished jigsaw puzzle on it? What if . . . ?

These are only a few examples of the sort of work you have to do in advance. Spontaneous sex requires a little forethought for it to work really well.

And what about you? Are you prepared? Have you changed, bathed, groomed? Do you have condoms ready if you need them? Nothing is worse for destroying sexual tension and excitement than one of the partners getting up halfway through to go and get something or disappearing off to the bathroom to brush their teeth. If you are planning a sudden seduction, remember that your partner may not be prepared, so let them have a few minutes at the start, just to check their hygiene or freshness.

You also need to check the ambience of the room you have selected for lovemaking. Is it suitable for love? Are the curtains closed if you have nosy neighbors? Do you both feel safe in it or do you fear the children suddenly interrupting you? Is the music and lighting suitable? Do you both feel relaxed and sexy? These things are important if you want to take your lovemaking from the ordinary to the extraordinary.

People sometimes think that the effort isn't worth it or they don't have time, and this is transmitted to lovers as they aren't worth it. The more effort you make to get the surroundings intimate, sensual, and arousing, the more your partner is going to be prepared to be intimate, sensual, and arousing with you.

You have to take into account your lover's tastes and preferences if you want truly ecstatic lovemaking. While you might think it fine to have sex after a cup of tea and a quick fondle, they may prefer a candlelit supper for two, exquisitely cooked and served with fine wine, then a very long, lingering session of intimate foreplay on a sensual wool rug in front of an open fire—and coffee and croissants and a red rose in a fine glass vase on a tray in bed for breakfast the next morning, while you might like to get up quickly, open your mail and dash off to work.

We are all different and want different things. By being considerate to your lover's needs you will find your lover much more likely to indulge all your passions rather than appearing cooperative but in reality feeling rejected by your lack of attention. The more you do, the more you get: that isn't a selfish or self-centered attitude—it's a fact. You have to invest time and trouble in setting the scene for some raunchy, madly passionate nights (and days) of love-making—or be prepared to accept second-best.

We all want to be pampered and worshiped, and setting the scene is preparing the temple for your lover's divine body to be adored.

If you want to take your lovemaking and sexual excitement to new heights of passion and raunchy lust, you have to think a little about when and where you have sex with your lover.

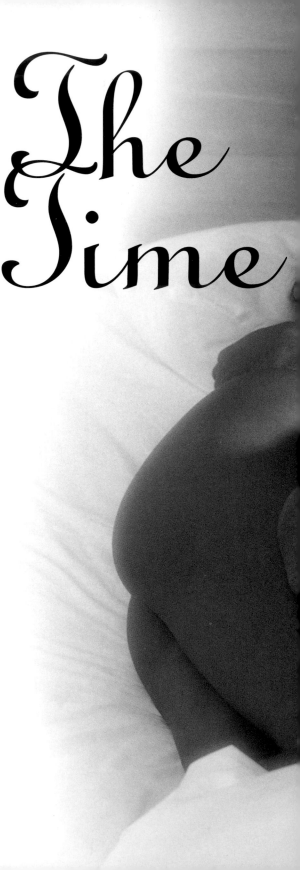

The Time

How is your sex life generally? Are you happy with it? Does it fuel you with enthusiasm and intrigue? Or are you bored and just going through the motions? If you are bored, it could well be that you are suffering from lack of choice or too much routine. The first thing is to decide if you are happy with what you've got; if not, you can start to make changes. The first and best change is *where* you make love. All too often it is the bedroom once you're unsuitably tired after a hard day's work.

Sex is special, erotic, sensual, recharging, passionate, important, and very seductive. If you only make love in the same place you sleep, you are relegating it to the same effect as a cup of cocoa—nice to have last thing at night and good for getting a restful night's sleep. But is it exciting? How much better to take some time to try to change this regular location. What's wrong with the kitchen? Or the bathroom? The car? The backyard? In a hot-air balloon? On a train? A boat? In a box at the theater? In the woods? In the fields? On the landing? If sex with your lover is an important part of reaffirming your love, then you owe it to them to make full use of other places to make love.

and Place

The same is true of the time you choose to have sex. All too often it is last thing in the evening when you are both tired after a busy day. So what's wrong with first thing, when it could really charge you up for the day and put a smile on your face all day at work? Or in the middle of the night? You could try setting an alarm clock and then waking your lover up by gently caressing them out of deep sleep into your arms.

If the only time you really do have is in the evening then what's wrong with making love earlier on? Why do you have to wait until you go to bed? It might be better to turn off the television and con-centrate on some real entertainment instead. Why not indulge in a little sexual excitement right then and there, in front of the television, on the living room floor?

One of the best ways of improving the location and timing of lovemaking is to discuss with your partner what they would like to try—you might be pleasantly surprised at the fantasies your partner has about lovemaking. There may be a few places— and times—that you hadn't even thought of. If some of them seem unusual or even bizarre—well, why not? Give it a try and you might find that you also enjoy it there and then. Your partner might suggest making love very late at night on the still-warm hood of the car after you've been out for the evening and it's just been parked in the driveway. You might think this shocking or risky but do it anyway because if your partner fancies it you owe it to them to try it. And you owe it to yourself to be more open and ready to exper-iment with your lovemaking—that's how to really experience seduction.

If you want a sudden seduction to work really well, you simply have to do some planning beforehand. It's no good springing it on your lover and expecting them not to be shocked or surprised— you have to give them some warning.

ONE OF THE best ways to give your lover some warning is to tell them—it really is as simple as that. Perhaps you could tell them in advance that at such and such a time you will be coming to see them and are going to make love to them wherever they happen to be in the house—without speaking, without any preamble or foreplay, without any removing of clothes, just pure and simple lovemaking. That should do the trick. They can then prepare themselves and be ready for you.

This technique works extremely well if you are both up for it. One of you may go out to work and you can say that one night this week, when you come home, you'll make love to them right there in the hall without any further ado. Leave it until later in the week and by then the sexual tension and excitement should be heightened. Your partner won't know which night you have planned the sudden seduction—and will expect it every night. When it does happen, they'll be eager because of all the delicious anticipation.

Sometimes just a little warning might be all that is needed. Suppose one of you puts the children to bed while the other does the dishes and makes the coffee. The one doing the chores can say that when the other comes down from reading bedtime stories, or whatever, then you'll make love right there on the kitchen table. Those stories will be read quickly that night!

Sudden seductions can also work well if neither of you knows when it's going to happen. You can try setting an alarm clock at random—when it goes off you make love. Or, when a certain word is said on the television in the evening, you'll both rip each other's clothes off and make love; if the word isn't said, you must wait until the next night. This technique makes you listen to what is being said on the television a lot more carefully. You can pick a word at random by just opening a dictionary.

You can also make a date for a sudden seduction. Pick a day at random in your organizer and a time, then close the organizer and forget about it. Until, that is, when the day comes and you both open your organizers and there it is.

Sudden seductions work only if you are both really up for it. They don't work if one of you isn't in the mood or has a low libido at that moment. They certainly don't work if one of you is tired, irritable, busy doing something else, or preoccupied. You have to be able to read your partner's mood pretty well. You should both also not have expectations that are unrealistically high. The scenes in movies where a couple has sudden and furious sex in a doorway are contrived. In real life it's less likely to work. There will be interruptions from people passing by, fumbling over clothing, being uncomfortable, feeling silly or too exposed, and it'll probably rain, which, unlike in the movies where it is sexy and fun, in reality it's merely wet and cold.

Men probably respond better to sudden seductions than women, who seem to need a longer time to warm up. Men, on the other hand, are usually delighted by sudden and unexpected sex. Again, you both need to know each other well and to be accommodating.

One good technique is to have a certain time—perhaps once a week—when you know in advance you are going to have raunchy rude sex and then you can both look forward to it knowing that there will be no long drawn-out foreplay—just getting down to it.

Booking into a strange place such as a hotel can get the juices running pretty hot as well. There is nothing better for sexual excitement than getting out of a rut and having sex somewhere new. You could book separate rooms and pretend to be complete strangers or try any other role-playing games you fancy. You can flirt like mad with each other over dinner—or with the waiters and waitresses—safely knowing that it will be with each other you will be having sex later. You could try having sex in the elevator as you go up to your rooms—but don't get caught.

Like sudden seductions, planned seductions need, well, a little planning. There is nothing quite so sexually exciting as knowing that you are both going to make love — but only after you have spent a little time getting to know each other again.

Planned Seduction

WHEN YOU FIRST meet your lover you spend a lot of time planning the seduction. You take them out or get taken out; you dress provocatively and well; you spend time and money on grooming and bathing. You want to look, smell, and be your very best for them. They, too, want the same for you. Once you have been together a while, it is all too easy to settle into a routine whereby you forget the excitement once generated merely by being in the same room together. Your lover becomes your partner. Where once you couldn't wait to get your hands on them and rip their clothes off and make passionate love to them, you become staid and accepting of second-best.

To rekindle those fires of passion and sexual excitement takes a little work but it is worth it. All you have to do is return to the same respect and admiration you once had. Take them out again. Spend time with them. Wine and dine them in a seductive atmosphere. Dress provocatively again for them rather than lazing around in any old thing.

Where once you invited, you now merely expect your lover to accompany you. Try inviting again. Suggest an expensive supper out—just for the two of you. Suggest that you'll make love again like you used to. Suggest anything you want—but be respectful and don't assume anything; in other words, behave as you

24

did when you first met. The secret of real sexual excitement is uncertainty. If you know for definite in advance what will happen, it removes the tension and thrill from the seduction.

By returning to the uncertainty of the first seductions and lovemaking you also return to the thrill of sexual excitement. Planned seductions have to be exactly that—planned. You might like to think that you're both going to make love after going out for dinner but if there's a little doubt, a little *frisson* of tension, it makes it all the more interesting, all the more exciting.

This uncertainty can also extend to touch. If you always fondle and caress your lover in the same way, they'll know what to expect, and will hardly feel excited. If you vary your caresses, they'll never know what to expect—and thus the sexual tension is heightened. If you have dinner together and always talk about your work or the children, they'll be blasé about it, but if you talk about when you first met or your first lovemaking, or how you felt the first time you saw your partner naked, or the first time you had an orgasm with them, they'll be intrigued and much more attentive to what you are saying. Talk to your lover about the sexual excitement that used to exist between the two of you and see if it can be regenerated.

Sudden seductions are about raw and lusty sex, whereas planned seductions should be more intimate, loving, gentle, more personal and tender. A planned seduction is a mark of great respect for your lover; it shows you care, that you have taken time and trouble over them, that they are worth your efforts, and that you don't just expect them to make love with you without any consideration for their feelings.

One technique that works extremely well to revitalize sexual excitement is to plan a once-a-week (or a once-every-two-weeks) date when you will spend a whole evening together (or afternoon, if you prefer) just making love. You can select the evening together and then one of you can choose what sort of lovemaking—raunchy, intimate, loving, tantric (see page 124), tactile, dressed or undressed, fantasy-orientated or not, whatever you like. The other person can then choose the next time. This way you'll both be able to get what you want and know you are pleasing your partner. Perhaps the one not choosing the type of sex can choose the venue or be responsible for preparing an exquisite meal for you both. This can work very well because both of you will be participating in an equal way; the onus on generating excitement doesn't fall on one partner alone, nor is one partner left feeling unfulfilled because their sexual needs haven't been met. As the time approaches for the planned seduction evening, the tension grows because you both know what is on the menu but not how it is to be cooked. Bon appeti

When we want sex, or are interested in having sex, we send out signals to our partner, either consciously or unconsciously. If you want to be an expert lover, you need to be able to recognize and pick up on these unconscious signals—the conscious ones are a lot easier to interpret.

Seductive

WATCH YOUR LOVER'S eyes during sex and you will see some enormous changes take place. Their pupils will dilate as they become more sexually aroused and the whole eye will widen. If you notice this enlarging of the pupil while you are caressing your lover or even just holding their hand it may be an indicator that they are getting sexually excited, or at least becoming aroused in some way.

Similarly, the skin will change as sexual arousal occurs. Your lover's natural scent may even change as the excitement increases and perhaps even before you begin to make love.

Some lovers have evolved complicated rituals of loveplay where they both know exactly where they

Symbolism

are with each other by what they wear to bed, or don't wear. How well do you know your partner's routines? What sort of clothes do they wear when they are trying to tell you that they are thinking sexually about you? Have you noticed any physical changes that they may undergo if they are planning to seduce you, or encourage you into bed?

Of course, the reverse may also work, where you can tell when your partner isn't sexually responsive by their body language, what they wear, or the tiny physiological signals that may be missing because they aren't sexually aroused.

By watching and learning from your partner you can understand their sexual needs better. Learn to use the lover's codes to enhance your lovemaking and seduction techniques, not to signal to your partner that you are too tired or too bored, or merely indifferent to their sexual wants and needs.

Talk to your partner about this and see if there are any codes you are using that may be detrimental to a good sex life, then you can substitute beneficial codes that tell each other that you are sexually responsive and willing. You can dress up for bed—that is always a good signal—or perhaps have a warm, soothing bath before bed to signal to your partner that you have refreshed yourself for them to enjoy.

Some couples go through elaborate signals— dinner out, seats at the theater, bunches of flowers, an expensive bottle of wine. All these are fine as long as both partners have agreed that the signal is just that—a signal. It is the merest hint of an invitation so that the other partner can back out gracefully if they aren't in the mood, or respond if they are. And like all good invitations there should be an RSVP—a chance

for another signal to be sent out in code to say what is acceptable—furtherance of the sexual encounter or a mild and kind declining of the offer.

Sometimes, in a long-term relationship, it's easy to overlook how simple the signals were when you first met. You didn't need any complicated language then—a merest glimpse of silk stocking or the putting on of a shirt and tie was enough to signal that you were getting dressed and ready for your lover. When you were first seduced you concentrated on each and every flutter of an eyelid; you watched your lover intensely. Once settled, you forget the subtle signals. The art of seduction is to remember how you responded then and rekindle that attention and observation once more, and thus relight the fires of passion.

Touch

We all like to be touched. Without touching we become withdrawn and depressed. Touching makes us stay——in touch. When we touch each other we are sharing an intimate and very personal act that enables us to pick up clues, read signals, and ascertain responses. Without touching, we are cut off from one of our most important senses and that deprives us of so much essential information that we become emotionally crippled.

The next sections look at all the delicious and sexy ways you can touch your lover——from kissing to caressing, from licking to sucking, from stroking to tickling.

33

Kissing

Kissing is a way of sending out, and receiving, signals about how ready you and your lover are for sex. Moist hot lips say more than words ever can and you should be eager and receptive enough to read these signals.

Kissing shouldn't be restricted merely to fore-play but should be an essential and exciting part of your lovemaking sessions. When you make love, try deep kissing your lover and exploring their mouth and tongue, especially as you and your partner come to a climax. Discover the sexual sensations as you suck hard on your lover's tongue just as they reach their orgasm.

After sex, passionate kissing can subside to the warmth and love of more gentle kissing, but it shouldn't stop altogether; keeping the kissing going can rekindle the second wave of lovemaking faster than anything else.

Kissing shouldn't be limited to mouths alone. Kissing every part of your lover's body is an essential part of good seductive techniques. There is absolutely no taboo territory for kisses—hands and fingers, buttocks and backs, rude bits and not so rude bits. And kisses can be many different things—moist nibbles, deep sucking, licking, biting (gently

of course), with lips, with tongues, wet and hot. Try kissing your lover in places you have never tried before—between the fingers or toes, along the backs of thighs and knees, behind the ears, on the bottoms of feet. You can kiss whatever bits you like and whatever bits your lover wants you to kiss—you and your lover may discover erogenous zones you never knew you had!

Our lips are very sensitive and they need to explore skin and other lips in order to be truly satisfied. Try kissing each other and pushing your fingers into your lover's mouth so they can suck on your fingers; try sucking hard on each other's tongues to feel the excite-ment that this can generate; lick each other's faces as you kiss and don't forget any bit—the eyelids, the ears, the forehead, the chin, and the throat are all especially sensitive to kisses.

Keep kissing at all times. Whether your kisses are filled with passion or are soft and gentle, it is through kisses that you express love as well as send out those seductive signals that all lovers want to receive.

Touching

Lovers need to touch. By touching you stay in contact. By touching you reaffirm your love and commitment. Touching doesn't have to be sexual. Holding hands when out walking is a way of being together, closely, all the time, and is wonderfully reassuring.

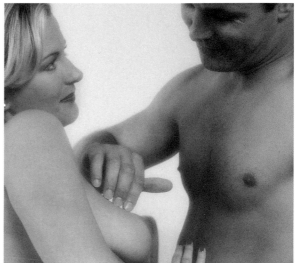

$\mathcal{T}$OUCHING MEANS SETTING the mood of love and seduction all the time without it being overtly sexual. If you don't touch naturally and spontaneously during the day, or when you are together, then the sudden touching of lovemaking can seem abrupt and discourteous. By the lightest stroking we send messages to our partner. It might be the softest touch of a hand on your lover's back or the gentle stroking of their arm while you are talking to them, but it all counts. Your lover will know that you are there, and there for them alone.

When you are making love, touching should go on as much as possible and shouldn't be restricted to the erogenous zones. Try stroking your partner's face as you make love and see the electrifying effect it can have.

After you have made love, keep touching, keep stroking. By keeping up physical contact, it reassures your partner that you didn't only want them for sex but also because you love them, value them, and want to stay in contact all the time. What better way of sending out a signal of love? The more you touch, the more you find out about your partner—their responses, their needs, their desires. The fingertips are incredibly sensitive, not only to pressure and feeling but also to finely tuned sensations that you would miss if you didn't touch. There is an almost telepathic quality to couples who touch a lot, as if they are so in-tune with each other that they are communicating on a very deep level—without words.

If you are aware that you and your partner don't touch, then try doing so. At odd moments during the day or evening reach out and stroke your partner in a nonsexual way and see the effect. Without making love, try touching each other all over and finding out which bits your partner likes you to touch. Try different pressures of touching and see how their responses change. Try stroking, teasing, light flicking with the fingers, caressing, tickling, and massaging.

Caressing

If you've ever seen holy statues, you will have noticed
bits worn smooth where the faithful have lovingly touched
their venerated object. Your lover should be worn smooth
all over with your touches as well. Your lover's body is
your temple and you worship it with your hands and lips
and love. Caressing is seductive. Caressing is gentle
stroking to keep in contact. Caressing can take place
at any time, anywhere.

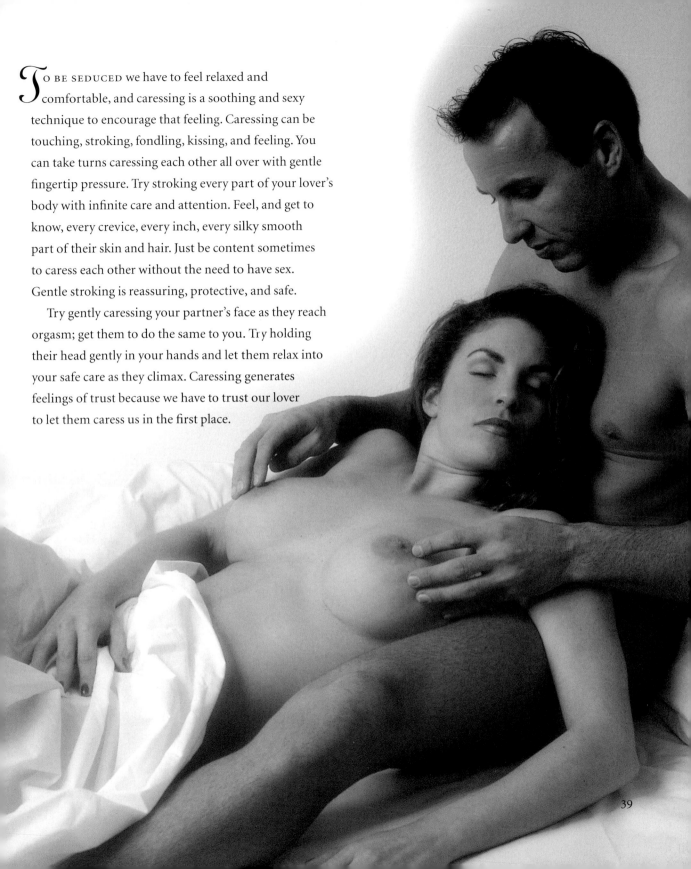

To be seduced we have to feel relaxed and comfortable, and caressing is a soothing and sexy technique to encourage that feeling. Caressing can be touching, stroking, fondling, kissing, and feeling. You can take turns caressing each other all over with gentle fingertip pressure. Try stroking every part of your lover's body with infinite care and attention. Feel, and get to know, every crevice, every inch, every silky smooth part of their skin and hair. Just be content sometimes to caress each other without the need to have sex. Gentle stroking is reassuring, protective, and safe.

Try gently caressing your partner's face as they reach orgasm; get them to do the same to you. Try holding their head gently in your hands and let them relax into your safe care as they climax. Caressing generates feelings of trust because we have to trust our lover to let them caress us in the first place.

39

Erogenous Zones

In popular myth the erogenous zones are limited to the sexual organs but we all know that isn't true. The erogenous zones are those areas of the human body that are capable of being erotically stimulated.

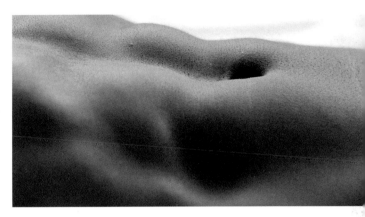

THE EROGENOUS ZONES are the erotic zones—
the areas to love and those areas that enjoy
being loved. Erogenous and erotic come from the
same Greek word—*eros*, love. For some lovers these
may indeed be the sexual areas exclusively but this
would be very rare indeed. We all have parts of us that
we simply adore being caressed and stroked, tickled
and licked. And your lover will also have
their own favorite bits.

So how many of your lover's erogenous zones do
you already know? How many of yours do they know?
If you don't explore and find out then you can't
improve on your seductive and sexual techniques. It is
true you could simply ask, but that wouldn't be quite
so much fun and, anyway, your lover may prefer you
to find out a little more practically.

When you are making love with your partner, try
exploring their body much like an early map-maker
would; chart each region; try kissing it; try licking it;
try stroking it; try tickling it. See what response you
get. You may think you know your lover's body pretty
intimately but you may learn new areas of delight
and new ways to please them.

They may well have areas that you didn't know
excited them, in ways you hadn't anticipated, but
which may come in useful later when you are devel-
oping and expanding your seductive techniques.
Perhaps there's a tiny area on the back of their neck
that doesn't respond particularly to touch but
when you blow gently on it, the effect is terribly erotic.

It seems to be generally true that women's and
men's erogenous zones are very similar, with obvious
differences for anatomical variations, but that they

have a different approach to having them touched.
Women tend to like a slower approach with more
caressing and massage first; while men prefer a more
straightforward approach. Women seem to be slower
to arouse and need more caressing, while men are
quicker and need more direct and immediate stimulation. However, everyone is different and you will both
need to experiment a little to find out exactly which
approach you both like.

With this information you are now ready to be
truly seductive. Your lover may be engaged in some
routine household chore but you know you can just
gently blow on their neck and drive them wild, get
them going, excite and delight them—and not even
have to get undressed, touch them, or do anything
else. Seduction indeed.

Skin

Once you realize just how sensitive skin is, you can play upon your lover's skin like a violinist. By gentle touch you can arouse passion and sexual excitement; the merest caress can drive your lover to heights of abandon.

A GREAT DEAL OF SENSITIVE information is sent to the brain from skin, which is densely packed with nerve endings. There are certain areas of skin that have more nerve endings and are more sensitive than others; for example, the fingertips have the most nerve endings of all. By simply caressing the skin on your partner's fingers—especially gently stroking the tips—you will be able to drive them wild with lust, if they are able to stand it. The soles of the feet are likewise well endowed with sensitive nerve endings, which is why they are such ticklish parts of the body. You can also use areas of the skin such as the fingertips, and hands in general, to make love to your partner in public without anyone realizing what is going on between the two of you.

Skin changes its sensitive properties under different circumstances, for instance, whether it is dressed or undressed, warm or cold, vibrant or tired. The parts of the body that normally have skin exposed are invariably the most sensitive areas—and thus the most erotic and teasable parts of the body.

You can arouse your partner's sexual desire to frenzied heights when you learn how to caress and tease those extra-sensitive areas of your lover's skin.

Bathing

Everyone likes to soak in a hot bath from time to time—and what could be more perfect than to be pampered while we are doing it? But first we must take care to prepare the pampering.

Spend some time preparing the bathroom to make it inviting and seductive. Candlelight is so much more evocative and sexy, so turn out all harsh electric lights and use only a lantern or candlelight. Perfume the air of the bathroom with your lover's favorite incense or aromatherapy oil. Prepare fresh hot towels for your lover to dry themselves afterward (or to be dried by you). Tidy the bathroom and put away all unnecessary things such as children's bath toys—this is about to become a room for seduction and love. Clean the bathroom—yes, the sink and lavatory as well—so that your lover feels special and welcomed by cleanliness. Change the floor mats, if you use them, so new or clean fresh ones are there for your lover's newly washed feet to walk on when they emerge from their warm and relaxing bath.

Run the water and make sure the temperature is just right for your lover—that might not be the right temperature for you, but you are doing it for your lover and what suits them goes.

Add a little drop of aromatherapy oil to the bathwater if your lover likes that. And you should now be ready to welcome your lover into the bathroom and provide them with such a sensual and sexy bath that they won't ever forget it.

Allow your lover to luxuriate for a while, soaking out the tension and stress of the busy day. When they have finished, you can dry them all over, gently, softly, and then lead them to the bedroom . . . perhaps a massage, perhaps soothing caresses, perhaps . . . You can make love in the bath with your lover—this can be especially good fun with lots of bubbles. Or you can just indulge in a little fun and games; for example, use the showerhead on each other's rude bits and see what effect it has. You can shower together and cover each other in hot suds and then spend quite a long time rinsing off all the soap suds—or even better try slowly and erotically wiping off the soap with your hands. And then you'd better make sure that each and every bit of your lover's body is completely clean by just lightly running your tongue over everything to see—and that does mean everything.

There is nothing quite so erotic as having your rude bits washed sensuously with a natural sponge lightly soaped; the sensations seem to be heightened with warm water and very gentle strokes of soapy circles.

Wash your lover all over with the softest of sponges. Wash their hair for them, bring them sweet fruit and fine wine. Allow them to soak and relax. Their bath should be for them to enjoy. The warmth and gentle washing will raise their libido.

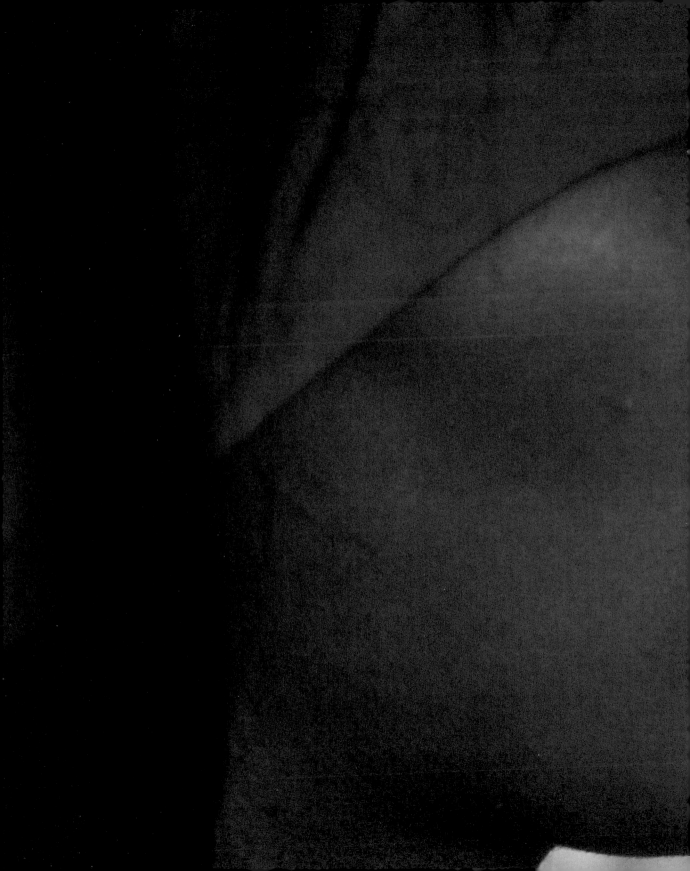

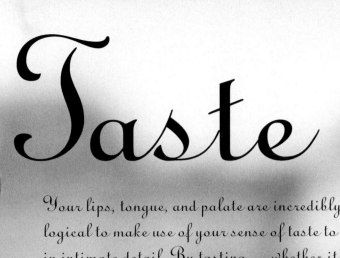

Taste

Your lips, tongue, and palate are incredibly sensitive, so it's logical to make use of your sense of taste to explore your lover in intimate detail. By tasting——whether it is food or skin——you experience oral-erotic sensations that are exciting and rewarding. In the next sections we will look at sexy foods and drinks, love potions, and aphrodisiacs, and, of course, the art of cooking rude food.

Foods

Food and sex have always gone together. The Roman orgies were as much about food as they were about sex. Food is essential to good seduction techniques. To prepare food for your lover and to eat a special meal together is intimate and seductive; it can also be erotic and lusty.

Some foods are more erotic and seductive than others; you wouldn't want to play sexy games with a steak dinner, but strawberries dipped in champagne and rubbed lightly across your lover's nipples and then eaten are certainly going to add to the sexual excitement.

In the West we have a certain reserve about eating food from each other's mouths but in the East it is considered highly erotic, and it is something you might like to try. You could suck cherries and pass them from each other's mouths as you kiss. Or, try eating asparagus with lots of butter—the bathtub may be a good place to do this.

Most fruit is sexy in some way because of the juiciness of it. Mangoes and figs have an especially erotic appeal—mangoes because they are very juicy and messy, and figs (fresh ones, of course) because they have a look of the vulva about them. A man eating, sucking, and nibbling on a fresh fig in front of his lover is certainly erotic, if done in the right way.

Experiment with taking different foods to bed and seeing what they taste and feel like when eaten off parts of your lover's body. A woman could try alternating between ice cubes and hot coffee as she fellates her lover. And the man could playfully use a peeled banana as a love toy and then slowly eat it—be careful it doesn't break off inside the woman.

There are all sorts of foods that lend themselves to cunnilingus—cucumbers, carrots, and certain chocolate bars, to think of a few—perhaps your imagination

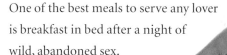

will come up with a lot more. And, for fellatio, there are a whole range of foods that create interesting and stimulating sensations—ice cream, honey, yogurt, warm runny chocolate; it's an ideal way to have a feast and please a man, but beware of piling on the pounds.

Honey, yogurt, cream, and ice cream all drip delightfully across nipples and mingle messily and erotically amongst pubic hair—just crying out to be licked off again.

You could take squishy food into the bath together and smear it all over each other's naked bodies, then slowly eat it all off—tomatoes, blackberries, avocados, chocolate sauce, or whatever you like to eat that makes quite a nice mess.

But perhaps the most erotic way to use food is to make it special. Knowing your lover's favorite foods is a way of being close, and they will be flattered. You could serve your partner dressed in nothing more than an apron. Choose their favorite wines to accompany the meal and they will be pleasantly surprised. One of the best meals to serve any lover is breakfast in bed after a night of wild, abandoned sex.

Drinks

To get you in the mood, drinks
don't have to be alcoholic, they
merely have to be sexy. In fact,
alcohol and sex probably don't
mix as well as some people think;
a little is fine but performance
decreases as consumption goes
up—moderation is the key.

So what makes a sexy drink? It's probably fairly obvious but advertisers would have us believe otherwise. The phallic shape of the bottles of some fizzy soft drinks may look right but the contents may not be as erotically charged as we are led to believe. A glass of champagne, however, is always sexy but a bottle of champagne is an excuse for a party and would render you unable to be really seductive—best stick to a glass or two. Cocoa may not be sexy but chocolate sauce is. Red wine is very sexy but then so is virtually any red drink that looks the same—blackberry cordials can have the same visual appeal if you want to keep a clear head for more serious matters.

You might like to experiment making your own sexy drinks—lime milkshakes, very liquid yogurt with crushed strawberries in it, thin chocolate sauce, ice cream with a melted chocolate bar in it, fruit juices with lots of crushed ice.

Don't restrict drinks to being merely drunk. Drinks can be poured over and licked off. Tongues can be dipped in and the drink sucked off. You can share the drink and kiss and swallow together. Try dipping your fingers in the drink and lightly rubbing your partner's nipples with it—and then letting them suck it off your fingers. You can experiment with various drinks and fellatio—what effect does a fizzy drink have? Or a very cold one? Or warm ones like tea or coffee?

And don't forget each other's personal juices—semen can be drunk, as can the moist secretions from a climatic vagina. You can exchange saliva and swallow each other's. You can mingle the sexy drinks with each other's sexy secretions, sweat, anything as long as you are both happy about it and willing to try. You can try using each other's bodies as cups for drinks—drink from each other's armpits, palms of the hand, the vulva itself, belly buttons—whatever can hold a little liquid and you can get your mouth or tongue to.

A little alcohol can help you lose some inhibitions but too much and you also lose the enthusiasm, drive, and ability to do anything about sex. Too much alcohol is also not good for you or your body, so limit the combination of alcohol and lovemaking to an occasional treat rather than a regular thing. You can always create sexy drinks without the need for them to be very alcoholic—a drink made with a little champagne and lots of orange juice will have just as good an effect, if not better, than several bottles of beer and is so much more seductive. A very dry martini is seductive; several very dry martinis are not, they merely make you drunk.

Love Potions

To make your own love potions you have
to treat the subject with a certain respect
and ritual. A love potion served in a plastic
coffee cup simply won't work. You need a
ceremonial chalice—a special glass, or
goblet perhaps, that is used only for your
love potion and nothing else.

WHAT YOU PUT into your love potion is up to you, since only you know what you and your lover might like. You could, however, try the following recipe for an interesting philter (drink to excite sexual love).

Love Potion 1

2 cups (500ml) of milk
1 glass of white wine
a pinch of ground ginger
a pinch of freshly grated nutmeg
a little sugar
a squeeze of fresh lemon juice

Heat the milk until hot and add the wine. Stir in the ginger, nutmeg, sugar, and lemon juice. Serve hot.

A refreshing love potion for a summer's day when you picnic naked in the woods is mint and lemon grass tea with some juniper berries.

Love Potion 2

1 bottle of full-bodied red wine
3 tablespoons brown sugar
4 cloves stuck into a small orange
1 teaspoon allspice
1 teaspoon freshly grated nutmeg
3 sticks of cinnamon
orange slices, to serve

Put all the ingredients except the orange slices in a pan and heat gently for about 10 minutes. Strain and serve with the orange slices. Traditionally, a well-beaten egg was added to this love potion just before serving.

At one time, any exotic and new plant that was brought from the Americas to Europe was instantly regarded as an aphrodisiac— including tomatoes, potatoes, and tobacco for a while. Oysters have gained their reputation as an aphrodisiac by being visually erotic and making us feel healthier.

Aphrodisiacs

THERE IS A whole variety of things that have a reputation for being an aphrodisiac because of their shape—rhinoceros, stag, and narwhal horn—or because the animal or plant they come from has seemingly magical qualities—tiger bone, ginseng, mandrake, fat of the camel's hump, salted crocodile, the blood of bats, and licorice. Most of them don't work.

The ones that do work—such as Spanish fly and yohimbe bark—are fatal in large doses (and you never know what is a large dose until it's too late). Rhinoceros horn may work by irritating the urethra but that isn't the same as being seductive or erotic— it is merely being irritated. True aphrodisiacs work by their mental and emotional effect. If you believe them to work, they will, and unless you try you won't know.

Some aphrodisiacs work by replacing lost vitamins and minerals, which boosts your system and makes you feel healthier and thus more sexy. Oysters are one of these. They are high in phosphorus and salt, as well

as looking erotic. Mind you, anchovies have a higher vitamin and mineral content, but don't have quite the same effect somehow.

The safe, healthy aphrodisiacs you can try are honey, garlic, basil, ginger, ginseng, chilies, asparagus, aniseed, caraway, avocados, wheatgerm, and, of course, oysters. Research indicates that vitamin E may help to produce sexual vigor, and a deficiency of this vitamin may be one of the causes of impotence and sterility. Eat plenty of wholewheat bread and you may have the perfect aphrodisiac, but maybe it is not quite so appealing as eating oysters and buttered asparagus naked in the bath with your lover.

Good sex takes place between two consenting, conscious adults. Anything given to you or your partner that detracts from that isn't good sex and may well be illegal as well as potentially fatal.

The best aphrodisiacs are a healthy body, a lively mind, and a partner you desire and feel safe with.

Food Games

We saw earlier how food can be a sexy addition to your lovemaking and how making love doesn't have to be a serious business—there is time and space to have fun. What better combination than food, games, and better sex?

POURING GAMES ARE probably the best types of food games—cream poured over a naked stomach or nipples and licked off is very erotic—followed by games that involve squishing all kinds of sexy food into each other's skin.

Obviously, when it comes to sex games, some foods work better than others—some foods are definitely sexier and a lot more practical for playing rude games with. You wouldn't want to take a cabbage to bed with you, but a bowl of fresh strawberries, some chilled champagne, a little cream, and lots of laughter will certainly set the mood for lovemaking. Honey is good, molasses not so good; strawberries are fine, apples need a bit more imagination; ice cream is a sure-fire winner, mashed potatoes are not quite so sexy or erotic.

You will need to make sure that you can clean up after your food games as no one likes sleeping in crumbs or damp sugary patches. Alternatively, you could spread a large plastic sheet on the floor and really have some fun—add some yogurt, strawberry jam, honey, and ice cream and roll around on the floor making love in your own gooey, sticky food fantasy—what a lovely sensation!

You might like to try blindfolding each other then you can push different foods into your lover's mouth and see the reaction—or blindfold both of you at the same time and try feeding each other; it's messy but fun. You could prepare an exquisite banquet of all your favorite foods and invite your lover to join you—and then eat everything off each other's bodies; no plates or cutlery.

If you want to be really inventive, fill the bathtub with custard and make love in it (you will need your largest saucepans to make enough custard, and let the custard cool down first, of course) or let jello set in the bathtub and then have a wrestling match with your lover. Or try smearing each other with chocolate sauce and awarding a prize of an orgasm to whoever can lick the most chocolate sauce off, or to the one who makes the most imaginative chocolate patterns on the other's body.

Food has a sensual feel to it if used in sex games— smearing and pouring, licking and sucking off are all very erotic acts that can heighten your tempo and raise the stakes of sexual excitement. So be daring and inventive in your approach to food as a seductive technique.

Cooking

Two people trying to share a kitchen can be a nightmare. One person cooking, dressed only in a provocative apron while the other watches can be very erotic. There's something so terribly risky about cooking in the nude——all that heat and sensitive body parts add a hint of danger to raise the libido.

$\mathcal{I}$F YOU WANT to share the cooking, both of you should be dressed only in an apron, then you can combine cooking with food games—tasting the food as you cook it and seeing if it tastes better when eaten off your lover's body.

You need to be aware of the obvious dangers of being burned but perhaps you don't even need to use the stove—a salad prepared for your lover while you are completely naked and they are fully dressed can be seductive. However, a little covering up can be more suggestive.

You could try finding innovative ways to serve yourself. Perhaps you could lie on the kitchen table while your lover prepares a cold meal spread over you as the dish of the day. Or how about finding novel

ways to serve your rude bits to your partner—men often have an easier time of this one because it seems their serving suggestions are often more practical to carry out.

However, women can still find unusual and entertaining ways to present themselves; nipples surrounded by pineapple rings with a light topping of cream, perhaps? A pubic area delicately served with strawberries and ice cream? You can take turns being the chef and wearing only the apron while the other is fully dressed. You could eat with your fingers and you get to wipe them on your lover's naked bits. Or how about wearing silky dressing gowns, which you let fall open at appropriate moments so your partner can see what is on the menu later.

Sound

If you've ever watched a rude video with the sound turned off,
you will know how essential to lovemaking sound is——without it,
sex is just faintly ridiculous. In the next sections we will look at
how erotic sounds can heighten and intensify sexual excitement and
how you can best incorporate sound into your lovemaking——from
an ear-piercing orgasm to the relaxing and enchanting effect of
someone reading aloud to you, from unzipping zippers to what
sort of music is best to make love to.

Literature

Seductive literature is about erotic passion; it isn't pornography. It is delicate and arousing, restrained and subtle, and well written. Imagine both being naked on a window seat in the late afternoon sun while you read your favorite bits of erotic literature to each other. It's seductive and gentle.

A LOT HAS BEEN written by good writers about erotic love and lovemaking, and you should have no trouble selecting suitable passages to entertain and to arouse each other with. Reading aloud in bed before making love is a wonderfully relaxing experience—and also very seductive.

You could go back to classical literature for your inspiration such as *The Thousand And One Nights*:

"Thereupon she pressed him to her bosom and he pressed her to his chest and the two embraced and in an instant that which his father had given him rose up in rebellion and putting both hands to her flanks, he set the sugar stick to the mouth of the cleft and thrust on till he came to the wicket."

Alternatively, try a little classical Bible:

"Thy navel is like a round goblet, which wanteth not liquor: thy belly is like an heap of wheat set about with lilies. Thy breasts are like two young roes that are twins"

What you read to each other doesn't have to be pornographic—just erotic. The act of reading aloud has erotic overtones, especially if you are suitably dressed, or undressed, for the occasion.

Reading erotic literature to each other can also help you to explore fantasies together that you might be to shy or unwilling to carry out in reality, such as bondage or cross-dressing or both. You could try this passage from James Joyce's *Ulysses*:

"so will you be wigged, singed, perfumed sprayed, rice powdered, with smooth shaven armpits . . . laced with cruel force into vicelike corsets of soft dove coutille, with whalebone busk . . . your figure will be restrained in tight frocks, pretty petticoats, the frilly flimsiness of lace round your bare knees."

If you've ever watched the movie "10" starring Bo Derek and Dudley Moore you will know the erotic effect music has when they begin to make love to Ravel's "Bolero." Two people ice skating to the same piece of music may be fun and entertaining to watch but is it erotic? It's the same music but it has a different effect.

Music

USIC HAS AN incredibly profound effect for some people, especially when they are making love; and for others it has hardly any effect at all. But how do you know until you have tried making love to a musical accompaniment? What sort of music is entirely up to you but music can certainly "set the scene." It provides a sensual background to seduction and lovemaking, wrapping our senses in silky tones that soothe and inspire.

Music doesn't have to be a passive experience. You can play your favorite music tapes and dance for each other—half undressed of course— or with each other.

You can make your own tapes for lovemaking. Start off with slower tracks then make the later tracks more frenetic and faster. You could choose rock and roll because it has a hard driving beat or go for popular classical music such as Wagner or Vivaldi. There are many "New Age" tapes you can buy to give you the sounds of the ocean or wind in a forest— whatever turns you on.

The whole subject of how music affects us with its resonance is vast, but it is worth noting that Indian temple music was often used as a sexual encouragement by the Hindus, and we can certainly try different sorts of music to see what their effects are. These could include reggae, African drumming, sitar, or Hawaiian.

Give your partner a set of light headphones and some suitable mood music and then perform oral sex on them and see if it enhances their enjoyment and orgasm. They could then do the same for you. And the beauty of this arrangement is that you don't have to do anything while being made love to—just close your eyes and allow the music to engulf you completely while you enjoy your climax.

Music can raise lovemaking to a completely new and exciting experience; just make sure you don't suddenly need to change tapes or CDs at a crucial moment.

Of course, the most seductive of all is to play music to your partner. We might not all be gifted musicians but we can all strum something. You might only be able to make a few chord changes on a guitar or play only one tune on a flute—but that might just be enough; there is something terribly flattering about having music played to us.

Drumming is something we can all do—even just simple beats. And the sound of drumming sets up a deep resonance that can awake the sexual urges and passion deep within us. Try holding a drum and dancing naked in front of your lover, and see what effect it has. If you are both open and willing to try new experiences, it can work wonders and greatly enhance your sexual excitement.

Making Noise

OBVIOUSLY, FOR ANY of this to work, you have to make sure you don't feel inhibited by the children hearing you—or your parents or neighbors. You will need to be in a place where you are certain you can make as much noise as possible without offending anyone. Perhaps you could try being outdoors—in a forest, on the beach, up a mountain—and see how the sound is different.

You can also experiment with moans and whimpers, cries and sobs of pleasure. You can make different types of sounds as your partner reaches orgasm and see what effect it has—for instance, try whispering words of encouragement—or talking "dirty" as they climax. You could describe in detail exactly what it is that you are doing to them to give them so much pleasure.

Making noise during lovemaking can be very erotic and seductive if handled properly and if you are both aware of what you like and are prepared to try it.

The next time you have an orgasm listen
to the sounds you make——and those your
partner makes. Are these sounds loud,
explosive, and dramatic or thin, quiet, and
restrained? Once you are aware of how
quiet you are then you can practice making
more sound. When you reach orgasm, let
the sound out in great shouts of joy.

67

Natural Environment

Sex can be a very lusty animalistic experience but being in the bedroom is too close to being romantic or going to sleep. By being outdoors, you can indulge your fantasies of running naked through the woods or making love in the swirling tide on some romantic deserted beach. It will make you feel more alive and natural and help you let go of your inhibitions.

BEING OUTDOORS ALSO gives you the chance to really experience nature—the wind on your skin, the feel of grass beneath your buttocks, dead leaves beneath your lover's back. It means you can make more noise or be more passionate or even just have more fun.

There are obvious provisos to making love outdoors: make sure you won't get caught or offend anybody. However, using a natural environment doesn't have to mean making love; there are lots of circumstances when it is perfectly permissible to flirt, be seductive, fool around, fondle, and titillate—all without having to remove a single garment or upset any onlookers who may be nearby.

Being outdoors ought to be a romantic as well as erotic experience—there is something so natural about sunshine and wind on our naked bodies that speaks of a deeper love, a more pagan experience. You could try seducing each other over a romantic candlelit supper on the patio on a warm summer's evening, or get up really early on vacation and experience the surf on your naked bodies as you fool around at the water's edge.

You could try driving out into the countryside and finding a remote secluded location by a river or lake where you could enjoy a very rude and very seductive picnic.

Outdoors

Having made love in a natural
environment, you might like to extend
the experience and make love—
or at least be erotic and seductive—
anywhere outdoors that takes your
fancy. Be adventurous and daring,
exciting and seductive.

BEING OUTDOORS MEANS being anywhere that isn't actually in your house—subways, movie theaters (relive your youth and book a back seat), shopping malls (you'd be surprised how much you can get away with in the changing room of a clothing store), in a ski lift, a taxicab, an airplane, a train (especially an overnight express with sleeping carriage) or even just going for a romantic walk together across the fields or along the beach.

Lots of people have erotic fantasies about being seduced in cars—perhaps it reminds them of their first fumbled sexual encounters when they were teenagers. Why not go for a seductive drive and see how much you can do to each other. You may have to stop the car if passions get too heated because driving and orgasms are not compatible.

You could try seeing how much you can get away with at the theater; hire a box and wear your sexiest outfits and see what you both can get up to in the darkness. See how far you can go in an elevator between floors. Or, how about hiring a boat and

making love to the sound of the gently lapping water as you float on a tide of sexual passion?

You could build a hot tub in your backyard and delight each other on long summer's afternoons by soaking together, then running naked into a plunge pool before having sex on the grass and returning to the hot tub for your afterglow.

There is nothing that makes a relationship go stale as quickly as predictable sex. Liven it up with expeditions to find the best place to make love outdoors.

71

Erotic Sounds

There is probably no more erotic sound than your lover having an orgasm. However, there are many erotic sounds that can be used in a seductive way before sex has ever taken place.

THE MOST EROTIC sound is probably the human voice and you can use it to devastating effect on your partner to seduce them at unexpected moments. Try phoning them at work and just telling them in no uncertain terms exactly what you'd like to do to them, their body and their temperature. Whisper it all in a hoarse voice and the effect is even more passionate—especially if you catch them just as they are about to go into an important business meeting—or even better actually in the meeting.

The unzipping of a zipper is a deliciously erotic sound if done slowly enough. You could phone your partner and just let them hear that sound—they will be home before you've put the phone down. Or, how about the undoing of poppers, or buttons, or Velcro? All these items are seductive and erotic and can be used to turn your partner on.

The sound of silk being gently drawn over naked skin is erotic and creates tension and a mood for love. Satin can have the same effect—nylon just doesn't do it.

Even the sound of a running bath can be seductive if the bath is intended for both of you—and not for washing necessarily.

When you are making love experiment with making erotic sounds—the smacking of lips for a kiss can be enhanced with practice. And you can add an extra dimension to lovemaking by amplifying the sounds of licking and sucking. Give it everything you've got and make a lot of noise. You can also whisper words of encouragement to your lover, which some people find very erotic. When you are being made love to, make sounds to signal that your partner is finding the right places.

Laughter can be both a wonderful release from tension and also very erotic. Laughing in bed or making love together is a sign you both feel very comfortable with each other and relaxed. You could try tickling each other and giggling together. Or, how about just moaning—this can turn on a lover like nothing else.

Sight

It is always assumed that men respond more readily and more sexually to visual stimulation. However, most women would disagree with this. What is true is that a man might like a raunchier view of his lover than would a woman——but a woman still gets sexually turned on by the sight of her lover; he just needs to be dressed in tight jeans or a stylish suit rather than in the nude.

Art

You only have to look around any art gallery to see what effect the naked human form has had on artists and painters over many centuries. There is nothing lewd or rude about nakedness, and your lover nude can only represent everything wonderful that you feel about them. There is nothing obscene about nakedness and the only judgment is in the viewer.

You could try your hand at painting each other in the nude—the one posing is in the nude; the one painting doesn't have to be but it often helps and breaks down any shyness or inhibition.

You may think you are not very good at painting—but you don't need to be. Take your time, you aren't trying to produce a masterpiece. You don't have to do a full oil painting, some sketching will do. Get your lover to pose in erotic positions, get them to display bits you would like to see more of and then you can spend some time pretending to draw them.

You could take photos of each other in your sexiest poses. If you are worried about getting photos developed, use an instant camera. Set rules about the photographer being in charge and the poser not being allowed to argue too much, then you can set up silly, erotic, ridiculous, bizarre, or even just plain portrait photos—whatever takes your fancy. Creating a little art together doesn't have to be pornographic—indeed it shouldn't even come close to it. Just play around with art for a while and see what effects you get. You can combine it with other techniques in this book—lingerie perhaps and then take photos of each other in your sexiest clothes—or how about outdoor shots? Or in the bath? Or closeups of oiled skin? All very effective.

If the worst comes to the worst and you really can't paint, draw, or sketch, try putting the paint on each other. The sensuous feel of oozing colors over each other's naked bits can be very erotic and seductive. You could paint arrows pointing to your favorite bits—or write suitable quotations on the naughty parts. You can spread a plastic sheet on the floor and roll around in the paint together; or spread a huge piece of paper on the floor, cover yourselves with paint, and make love on it. Then you will have a permanent abstract reminder of a passionate moment. You could frame it and hang it on the wall—no one but you would know what it meant.

Lighting

Naked skin seen in all its full glory in the bright light of day can be a little daunting. We all have blemishes and bits we would prefer to hide, so make your lighting seductive and alluring and use it to make the best of what you've got.

NATURAL LIGHT IS fine when it is dimming and fading—evening twilight and early misty mornings. But when you haven't got the right sort of natural light, you can enhance it with a little help. The softer the lighting, the more seductive it is. Candlelight and firelight work best since they are natural and moving. They are also dimmer than electric light, helping to set the mood and hide some of the shortcomings.

If you haven't got either candlelight or firelight then soft lighting from table lamps is better than harsh overhead lighting—fluorescent strip lighting is even worse than daylight. You can change the colors of any shades you use on table lamps or bedside lights to see what moods you get from the different lighting effects, or you could use colored bulbs.

Despite what you may think, red lighting isn't actually the most erotic. It can seem a little seedy and it also alters skin tones to make them appear artificial and fake, and it is often reported that it can make lovers feel irritated, even angry.

A pale orange or amber is better. The best lighting for setting a seductive mood might well be a cool tone of green or blue. These colors have the effect of making the skin seem fuller and more radiant.

A purple light is worth trying because the effect on the sexual organs is quite extraordinary—it seems to amplify them and make them very much something to focus on. The Indian tradition of sexual Tantra (see page 124) often suggests purple light to encourage female sexuality to blossom.

You could try combinations of lighting—a bright green with a more vibrant but dim red may be the best combination—but find your own best choice.

You could hire a strobe light and do a sexy striptease for your lover—or get them to do one for you. This works just as well if you hire an ultraviolet light—make sure you wear lots of white clothes because they show glow in the light and can be very erotic. Your lover won't see much of you but the sight of your white underwear dancing will turn them on.

Whatever lighting you go for do it dramatically and tastefully. There's nothing quite as off-putting as poor lighting or a bare bulb. This goes for the best lighting of all—candles—just as much. One white household candle does nothing. But imagine the effect on your lover of a hundred candles lighting your boudoir. Making love by candlelight is an unforgettable experience and, once done, will need to be repeated—often.

Lingerie

Technically, lingerie means women's underwear and it comes from a French word meaning linen. However, today lingerie tends to be sexy underwear, worn by either men or women, that is something more than their normal everyday underwear. Lingerie is worn for taking off when making love—not to keep your rude bits warm in the winter.

CHOOSING LINGERIE SHOULD be done by both partners: it is all too easy to choose something inappropriate for your partner by yourself. Men make the obvious mistakes in this area since they do like to pick sexy garments that are a little too tarty for their partner's taste. Department stores are full of men buying such items just before Christmas—and equally full of women changing them just afterward.

If you shop for lingerie together, it also provides an exciting opportunity for some more fun—see what you can get up to in the changing room together. Lingerie is designed to be sexy—not coarse. So choose items that flatter and conceal rather than cheapen and reveal. Crotchless panties may figure in a lot of men's fantasies but they really are rather too much for most women. Lingerie works best when it is made of the finest fabrics—silk is good; nylon not so good. It should be wispy and alluring; tantalizing and fun; demure but sexy; provocative but classy.

And it doesn't only have to be of silk or satin—most women report that they think their lover looks best in plain but tight white cotton boxer shorts; designed to outline everything but reveal nothing. Lingerie, as separate from normal everyday under-wear, should be kept for seduction and lovemaking. Once you start wearing it all the time it can lose some of its appeal—especially for your lover; if they see you in it all the time they won't be able to read it as a signal when you do wear it for sex.

Lingerie should be special, which means you can really go to town on it. You can wear items that might be too expensive for everyday use—or too extreme or bizarre. You could, for instance, invest in a really old antique bone corset that laces up tightly at the back, or how about Victorian silk underwear—you wouldn't want to risk wearing that every day but it might be very pleasing to your lover if you wear it on special occasions, for them to know how much you value them and their excitement.

Dress for your Lover

We all have to wear clothes, most of the time, and some of them are reserved for special occasions——a business suit for going to work, a set of overalls for fixing the car, a warm coat for winter walks——so it makes sense to have certain clothes set aside for seducing your lover——things you know turn them on and get their pulse racing.

I F YOU DO set aside certain clothes only for seduction and loveplay, these clothes can be extravagant and extraordinary—better than anything you would normally wear. You may like to use them as signals for lovemaking—when you wear a certain item it reminds your lover of the great times you've had in the past when you wore it.

Taking time to dress up for your lover makes them feel good because you've made so much effort purely for them, and the fact that you're wearing something really special is significant to them. Dressing for your lover doesn't mean wearing tarty or revealing clothes—quite the contrary. You can wear clothing that is elegant, refined, and luxurious, purely because you are reserving it for special wear and not risking it by wearing it for everyday use. It might be best to choose items that unzip or undo easily, but that is a personal preference; your lover might like something that is much harder to get you out of. Sometimes it is more sexy and seductive to have to work really hard to

get to your lover's interesting bits, and any barriers put in the way, such as zippers, poppers, and buttons, can make the experience even more delicious. Lots of people like to be undressed very, very slowly. It is both erotic and tantalizing, and it also sort of suggests that they are valued and worth taking time over.

Dressing up for lovemaking is a bit like dressing up for the theater or a movie—yes, people used to do that in the old days. It makes a special occasion even more special. There is nothing quite so seductive and erotic as seeing your lover prepare themselves—and you both knowing what is to come later. You can give your lover quite a thrill by slowly dressing in front of them—not allowing them to touch, until later of course. You could both try dressing each other— no touching, though—and see if it's as exciting as taking the clothes off each other again later.

You could have a variety of outfits to wear, each one signaling something different. Perhaps you could save the very best, the most elegant, for when you want gentle, affectionate lovemaking—and wear ripped jeans for when you want a quickie on the kitchen table.

Undress for your Lover

When we get ready for bed to go to sleep we take our clothes off and put them away——or just drop them on the floor——but we do it casually and without thought. Undressing for our lover is a totally different thing and must be carried out carefully and with a great deal of thought.

You have to be aware of what effect undressing has—does your lover like total nudity or prefer some things hidden? Would your lover be turned on by a full striptease or simply find it humorous? Would the occasional flash of something naughty revealed beneath a full-length coat be more of a turn-on than seeing you totally nude?

When you undress for your lover, remember that the whole atmosphere is as important as the fact that you are taking your clothes off. The lighting must be right. You also have to think about creating the right mood with music, aroma, comfort, and surroundings. Taking your clothes off while your lover is finishing breakfast in the harsh light of a sunny day might just work, but on the other hand it might be better if you

pulled the blinds down first and created a more seductive atmosphere with suitable music playing.

Undressing can be erotic if handled properly or a turn-off, if not done properly. It's best to be a little discreet—tantalizing glimpses are more erotic than total nudity; a quote about a famous French courtesan, Colette, was that "when she raises her eyelids it's as if she were taking off all her clothes." Sometimes you can do more with a look than with total nudity.

On the other hand, sometimes total nudity can be exactly what the situation requires. Perhaps your lover is on the phone and not paying you any attention. Walk through the room completely naked and then disappear—the chances are your lover will come and find you pretty quickly.

For centuries women—and men—have adorned their bodies with makeup to make themselves more alluring and sexy. Nothing has changed. A little makeup can enhance the plainest of faces and give us sexy clues as to what is on the person's mind.

Makeup

It REQUIRES ONLY one thing for makeup to work effectively—to be different. If you are a woman who goes out to work everyday wearing lots of makeup, experiment by not wearing any at all for your lover—the fresh scrubbed look of a clean face may work wonders. Similarly, if you never wear any makeup, experiment with lots of it for once and see if it has a seductive effect on your lover.

Seductive makeup is about changing your appearance, not hiding it. It is about making you look like someone else occasionally—rather than trying to make you look better or more glamorous—although, of course, it may do this incidentally.

Makeup for men, with its effeminate overtones, may have had a bad press in the past but, done well, it can be very alluring and sexy. If the man wants to experiment with his lover's makeup, it is best if she helps him and puts it on for him initially. A little light eye shadow, a tiny touch of lipstick can make quite a difference and help to blur conventional boundaries and break down stereotypical role playing. Once we break through such barriers, our lovemaking can be on a much more equal footing—and all this accomplished with a little mascara.

Makeup for loveplay shouldn't be restricted to the face alone. Try applying rouge to each other's nipples and see what a heightened sexual effect you get. Draw sexy diagrams on each other's belly or draw arrows to the bits you like best.

Makeup can also be used to dramatic effect to change your character completely—you only have to think of the dead-white makeup of the Japanese geisha girls with their blood-red lips. Nowadays body piercing is taking the place of makeup but that is up to the individual and not to be recommended as a seduction technique.

Smell

Sometimes a smell—
especially the special
smell of a lover—can
haunt us for years.
Our sense of smell is so
acute, but so refined, that
we often overlook it as a
powerful seduction tool.

The sudden smell of a particular aroma can take us back to our childhood, or an early sexual encounter, so completely that it's as if we were actually back there. When Dante Rossetti wrote, "I have been here before. But when or how I cannot tell: I know the grass beyond the door, the sweet keen smell, the sighing sound, the lights around the shore." he knew the power smell can have; the delicious lingering perfume that reminds us of someone but who we cannot remember. We simply remember the smell, the heady scent, and we are transported. Our sense of smell is an important part of seduction.

Perfumes

No one needs to wear perfume nowadays to cover up body odor. We can all smell sweet and clean without perfume, but we all continue to use it in some form or another. We might call it eau de toilette or some other fancy name—aftershave, aftershower refresher, eau de cologne—whatever. Once you accept that perfume is the smell of sex, you can start to have fun with it.

RATHER THAN JUST using the same perfume, day and night, experiment with different types and see what effect they have on your lover. Some perfumes are sharp and others sweet, some fragrant and others more chemical. And they all have a different effect. Some are so effective that lovers may become aroused merely by the smell. You will have to experiment a little until you get the desired effect. Knowing that your lover uses a particular smell to get you going can be quite a turn-on in itself—there's something terribly flattering about someone taking time and trouble just to please you.

Perfumes are usually alcohol based; the alcohol evaporates once on our skin, leaving behind the fragrance mixed with musk. Musk is the sexy bit. It comes predominately from the musk deer, extracted from their musk glands and processed. The musk deer's smell seems to affect us humans in a particularly pleasant way though no one really knows why. The more expensive the perfume, the greater the quantity of musk; manufacturers won't admit this and will tell you all sorts of things about the expense of producing a particular rose petal or some other flower for the fragrance. Truth is, it's the musk that turns us on.

Incense

Most people have at one time or another used incense to add a certain something to their home—either ritual and mystery or simply to provide a sexy seductive aroma—and maybe wondered where and how its use started.

PERHAPS IT WAS the earliest nomadic tribes who discovered that a handful of certain leaves sprinkled on the dying embers of a fire would produce a sweet smell that covered up the smells of stale food, or maybe they used aromatic plants in their cooking and when some fell into the heat of the fire they liked the pleasant aroma. We do know that the ancient Egyptians and Babylonians used incense as part of their religious rites, and in China it was used as a magic potion, a charm to counter hungry ghosts.

Traditionally, there have been two ways to burn incense. It can either be loose, sprinkled onto glowing charcoal, or it can be blended with charcoal and gum, and shaped into sticks or cones. The gummed incense needs a good draft to make it burn, which is why in religious ceremonies the incense burner is swung backward and forward to produce a moving current of air to help the charcoal to glow.

Whether you want to burn some incense to settle your own ghosts or to create a sexy atmosphere for seduction, there is nothing better than making your own. The following recipes produce aromatic incense that will soothe and seduce you and your lover and help to improve your lovemaking.

LICENTIOUS LOOSE INCENSE

1 oz. (25g) gum benzoin (from a pharmacy)
¾ oz. (20g) ground cardamom seeds
1 oz. (25g) powdered sandalwood
¾ oz. (20g) ground cassia bark
¼ oz. (15g) ground cloves

Blend all the ingredients together; you will find the gum acts as a fixative. The cassia can be replaced with ground cinnamon, if you prefer. You can add to the basic recipe a little freshly grated nutmeg, lavender, dried lemon or orange peel, bay leaves, or even a little cayenne pepper to give it added spice—that should warm things up a bit.

SEDUCTIVE CONE INCENSE

8 oz. (200g) charcoal
¼ oz. (10g) powdered sandalwood
¼ oz. (10g) ground cassia
1 oz. (25g) powdered gum benzoin
4 oz. (100g) gum arabic

Crush the charcoal finely and mix it with the sandalwood, cassia, and powdered gum benzoin. Mix the gum arabic with enough water to make a stiff paste, then stir it into the rest of the ingredients. Form the incense into any shape you want, such as cones or a nice phallic shape for added interest. Let it dry for a day or two before using. Again, you can add any other ingredients you like to this basic recipe.

Aromatherapy

Aromatherapy (the use of essential oils) may seem like a New Age invention but it has actually been around for many thousands of years. The ancient Egyptians certainly knew about the therapeutic and erotic qualities of certain essential oils.

Essential oils, when heated to give off an aroma or when mixed with oil or cream and applied directly to the skin, can have a deeply profound effect on people and, as such, are beneficial when it comes to enhancing lovemaking.

You can buy essential oils very easily these days at any good pharmacy. Most essential oils have healing or restorative properties but we are concentrating here on the ones that will arouse your passions—there are certain essential oils that are better for seduction than others.

It's best to heat the oils to give off their sexually arousing properties rather than applying them directly to the body. Essential oils work on a very deep level, they are not simply perfumes or incense but rather air that has been charged with almost magical qualities—the hypnotic power to set the right atmosphere for seduction and sexual excitement.

However, if you do want to make your own aromatherapy oil for applying directly onto your lover's body, you will need a good collection of essential oils (these should never be taken internally, by the way, without medical supervision or advice from a qualified aromatherapist). You will also need a base oil to mix them with. The base oil can be a very light one, such as grapeseed, or one with a very mild fragrance, such as almond. If you want a truly exotic oil, try coconut oil, which comes in solid form and melts in your hands—very erotic indeed. You need a ratio of roughly 3 drops of essential oil to 4 tablespoons of base oil. Using oils for massage is covered in more detail on page 109.

To heat essential oils you can either buy aromatherapy burners or try sprinkling a few drops of the oil straight onto a candle flame. Good oils to use are gardenia, lavender, rose, and jasmine.

Oils to generate lust and passion are neroli, ginger, ylang ylang, cinnamon, and basil.

If you want to create an atmosphere for seduction, try using musk, patchouli, sandalwood, and juniper.

Try a few drops of jasmine, musk, and ylang ylang for a truly evocative and deeply sensual smell.

You can, of course, make your own favorite oil by experimenting with different combinations. The secret with good aromatherapy is to use oils in moderation; air that is too heavy and heady with scent can be overpowering.

If your lover is feeling off-color you can help them by using aromatherapy oils. For headaches, use cardamom, lavender, rosemary, or pennyroyal. For depression, use bergamot, camomile, jasmine, sandalwood, or geranium. For a cold or flu, use cinnamon, basil, marjoram, or hyssop.

For a truly effective aphrodisiac, try a mixture of cardamom, jasmine, juniper, sandalwood, orange blossom, patchouli, ylang ylang, and rose. That should do the trick. And if you want to create a truly sexual smell in the air, which will have your lover ripping your clothes off as soon as they come through the door, blend 6 drops of essential oil of frankincense, 2 drops of essential oil of cinnamon, 6 drops of essential oil of orange, and 2 drops of essential oil of ginger—be cautious with this stuff, it's dynamite.

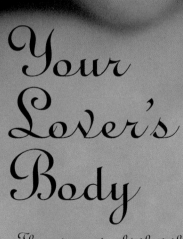

Your Lover's Body

There is no doubt that the sense of smell in human beings is declining. We no longer rely on it to warn us of danger or to sniff out food, but it is still there and is still working very effectively on a subconscious level.

ℰARLY SEX MANUALS rarely mentioned the sense of smell as a part of lovemaking, or if they did they recommended masking it or getting rid of it altogether. But we do give off a natural body aroma and the important thing is that it attracts a partner. The chemicals your body produces for this effect are called pheromones and they are very powerful. A male gypsy moth can smell the pheromones of a female from over three miles away. We are not moths, however, and our pheromones only work within a limited distance—probably not much more than a few feet. But they are powerful and they do send out subtle but effective signals. By washing and perfuming ourselves we mask these signals.

To most people the smell of a freshly bathed lover is preferable to a dirty, hot, sweaty one. But bathing does remove the pheromones and this can lead a lover to feel less turned on. Obviously you have to be clean for your lover but, while making love, smell each other intimately—provided you are both agreeable—and see if your lovemaking isn't enhanced by your lover's smell.

It may seem odd that we spend so much time masking our natural smells if they are so powerful, but we are in the grip of marketing here. The perfume manufacturers have to sell their products, and what better way than by convincing us that what nature gave us is not really satisfactory and that they can do better, and we can buy it. Modern pharmaceutical companies are, however, fully aware of the effect of pheromones and are now incorporating them into their perfumes and aftershave lotions.

For a few days, try using plain unscented soap to wash and bath with, and stop using perfume or aftershave, and see if your partner notices or responds differently to you. You may be pleasantly surprised.

In Chinese medicine, the smell of a person can lead to diagnosis of illness and, while we aren't in the business of detecting illness, we can still notice changes in our lover's smell and react accordingly. Sometimes your lover may have a different smell, which might indicate that they are more sexually turned on; how easy it would be to miss this interesting and rewarding signal if you didn't notice.

Sometimes just breathing in deeply the air around our lover's neck and then saying, "God, but you smell fabulous," can be a real turn-on for them. We all want to smell good and being told we do is very reassuring. But no one likes to be told the opposite, so be very diplomatic if you have to.

Flowers

Flowers are visually beautiful— but they also smell divine. They each have a unique smell that is instantly recognizable. Who cannot tell the deliciously delicate fragrance of a rose from the heady lusty smell of lilies? Flowers have been given by lovers to each other for centuries.

WHAT'S THE FIRST thing your lover does when you present them with a fine bouquet? Why, they bury their head in the flowers and breathe in deeply, taking in all that delicious natural perfume, and it tells them how much they mean to you. Not by the size of the bouquet, or by it's rarity value, or even by the fabulous arrangement. No, they know because of that smell. Each flower means something. The language of flowers is spoken without words. It is spoken in smells and fragrances, so be careful what you give.

If you give (or receive) bluebells, it is a sign of commitment and constancy. Camellias mean perfect loveliness. The rose is obviously the best one since it means quite simply "love." Tulips are a declaration of love, as yet unfulfilled; violets mean modesty; lily of the valley, a return to happier days (nice if you've just made up); daisies are for innocence; forget-me-nots for true love; honeysuckle means the person is ready to be seduced; lilacs for blossoming love; and daffodils for respect and gallantry. The ones to watch out for—especially receiving them—are anemones, you'll know you've been replaced; columbines, a lover thinks you are foolish; geraniums, a lover is sad (and probably ready to replace you); sunflowers, the person considers themself better than you; narcissus, the person knows that they're better than you; and iris, a lover is trying to tell you something.

Buy as many roses as you can afford (or even more if you really want to make an impression)—blood-red ones are best—and separate the petals. Spread them on pure white sheets, open a fine bottle of wine, bathe and prepare yourself, and then invite your lover to join you, making love on the crushed fragrance of pure roses.

You can garland each other's hair in flowers; float them on the water of your bath; or, better still, run naked through the woods filling each other's arms with them and making love on a bed of wild bluebells.

Herbs

The essential oils for aromatherapy come from plants, and most of these plants are easily available in their natural state. They are known as herbs and they have potent and interesting properties when it comes to increasing sexual excitement. Herbs have strong smells—and strong tastes, of course—and when crushed they give off their aroma to delight and arouse us.

Some herbs work best if they are fresh—
rosemary is a good example of this. Who can
resist the delicious smell of rosemary when it has been
added to roasting meat and served as a special meal
with a favorite wine. Some herbs, however, work best
if you allow them to dry first. You can then burn them
on an open fire and they will give up their aroma.

If you want to increase intimacy and love, try
burning apple wood, basil, jasmine, and lavender. If
you want to increase vigor and potency, try geranium,
mustard, peach wood, or poppy. For lustiness, try borage,
mullein, or yarrow. For staying power, try comfrey,
ginger, honeysuckle, or cedar. To increase allure and
attractiveness, try juniper, nutmeg, rue, or oak.

You can experiment with burning a few dried
leaves or small twigs of the herb or plant and see
which you prefer, and which has the best effect.

Herbs also have a very strong effect if eaten or
drunk. You can add some of the herb to oil for use
in cooking—and the beneficial effects should be just
as noticeable.

Herbs are well known for their medicinal effect and
if your love life is flagging because you are overtired or
depressed or just recovering from an illness or surgery,
then herbal remedies can certainly boost your vitality.
It is best to consult a qualified herbal practitioner
before attempting home diagnosis or treatment for
any conditions or complaints.

Herbs have many uses: you can use them to add to
aromatherapy oil (see page 94) for massage; make
incense with them (see page 92); use them in rude
cooking (see page 58); add a few drops of essential oil
made from herbs to your bath water to make a very
relaxing and refreshing bath (see page 44); or crush
them so that they release their natural aroma in the
room just before making love—you could try the
leaves of wild garlic for this, or rosemary, lemon grass,
mint, or dill. The Romans used to swear by lettuce as
a lust-making plant—a salad just before you plan to
make love seems like a good idea.

All the

We have looked at the individual senses separately in the previous sections——and had a little fun along the way increasing our sexual excitement. In the next section we will look at combining all these senses to create the perfect seductive and erotic sexual excitement—— and having some more fun. The first thing we need to look at is whether you and your lover have compatible libidos. If not, the following sections will give some helpful tips and techniques for getting it back on track.

Senses

Libido

Technically, your libido is your sexual urge and, unless you have no sexual urge at all, that's all there is to it. However, libido is often compared to someone else's; if they aren't compatible for whatever reason, one libido is called high and, therefore, the other must be low. If only it were that simple.

NY COUPLE WILL at some time experience a disparity of libido. One of the partners will want more sex and the other less. That is natural and quite expected. What is unnatural and unexpected is to put pressure on a partner, or have pressure put upon oneself, to have sex when one just plainly isn't in the mood.

A "low" libido may be expected owing to stress; or recovery from illness, surgery, or childbirth; or even just plain old-fashioned tiredness. But if regular sex isn't taken up again after the causes of low libido have been removed then it can become a habit to "do without." While that habit may be quite acceptable for one of the partners, for the other it may not be. Any relationship that is being conducted without the intimacy, release, and relaxation of good and regular sex needs examining. A short-term loss of libido should be expected to occur at some time; long-term loss of libido certainly needs examining and correcting.

Boredom and predictability are the chief enemies of a good sex life. If you always do what you've always done then you'll always get what you've always got. If you experiment, are adaptable and open to new ideas, are prepared to try anything—within reason—and are prepared to do some work then your relationship can only thrive and survive. If you stagnate, sexually, then so will your relationship.

A stagnating relationship may well be enlivened by the appearance of a "third party." But do you want to have an affair to restore a flagging sex life? If you can't work it out with the partner you are with, then what hope do you really have of working it out with someone else? You wouldn't trade in your car just because it had a puncture—you'd get it fixed. Low libido can be fixed if you are both prepared to work at it. A diminishing libido can sometimes be an indicator of something else wrong in a relationship, so before commencing work on restoring lost libido make sure you both are in love, willing to try, committed and happy with each other generally, then you can begin to restore lost sexual activity. If either of you has a problem with the relationship itself, you cannot hope to replace lost or diminished libido first.

The easiest way to restore low libido is to stop trying. Nothing makes libido vanish as fast as having a spotlight put on it. Once you think that libido should have a certain level you are doomed. It will vary from moment to moment. What you have to do is work at restoring intimacy, romance, seduction, closeness, warmth, trust, and togetherness. Once these things are in place the scene is set for sexual relations. However, that is a goal or destination. Libido works best if given a vague itinerary and left to wander about a bit on its own without pressure to arrive anywhere at any set time. Build up trust and confidence first. Spend time not having sex but having all the other things that surround it—massage each other, fool around a little, flirt, kiss, stroke each other, get to know each other again, have foreplay, hold hands, spend time together being silly and laughing, go for walks, enjoy each other's company without any pressure to have sex, and, most important, be in love. Once you remove the pressure, the lost drive will return.

From the moment we are born, we like to be touched. Touching, especially by way of massage, helps us to bond with our partner, soothes and comforts us, relaxes us, eases pain and muscular tension, increases our vitality, and improves mobility and flexibility— what could be better for better sex?

Massage

OBVIOUSLY THERE ARE many different forms of massage from very deep to extremely gentle and therapeutic, but here we are interested in the sort of massage that gets the blood moving, the pulse racing, the libido building, and the juices flowing—sexy massage for lovers.

If you're no expert in the art of massage, it doesn't matter. You don't have to know all the names of the muscles or even how to do a proper massage—oily erotic hands slipping slowly and seductively over gleaming naked flesh will arouse the passions and bring out the lust in your lover. So the first thing you need is oil—lots of it. The aromatherapy section

(see page 94) explains how to add essential oil to a base oil. Essential oils give a lovely smell as well as having quite a profound emotional effect. For your base oil, use a mineral oil such as grapeseed, sweet almond, or coconut. The best essential oil to add to it is a few drops of ylang ylang—this is known for its lusty effect. Always check the safety information on individual essential oils and test for allergenic reaction before using any new oil on the skin. Put a few drops on the back of the wrist, cover with a bandaid, and leave for an hour to see if any redness or irritation occurs.

You will need plenty of clean towels if you don't want oil all over your best rugs—or you could lay

down a large sheet of plastic and then have no worries at all, and plastic has quite an erotic quality to it if you both roll around it and oil yourselves together.

Sexual massage should be done gently and sensuously. You're not trying to ease aches and pains or correct posture problems—you're there to raise the erotic temperature. Most men like to be massaged but find it so erotically stimulating that they get erect quickly and want their erection to be held while their lover massages the rest of them with one hand. Women, on the other hand, seem to prefer to be massaged all over first before their naughty bits are attended to. You can see men and women as spirals of energy, with the man's spiraling out from his penis and the woman's spiraling toward her vulva. For men, their energy is central to their genitals and they need

them massaged almost immediately; for women, their energy needs to be focused and directed slowly and with the excitement building up gradually. But you will both have to experiment to find the right method for you as a couple.

The secret of giving a good massage— especially a sexual one—is confidence. Even if you haven't a clue what you're doing, act as if you do then your partner will be

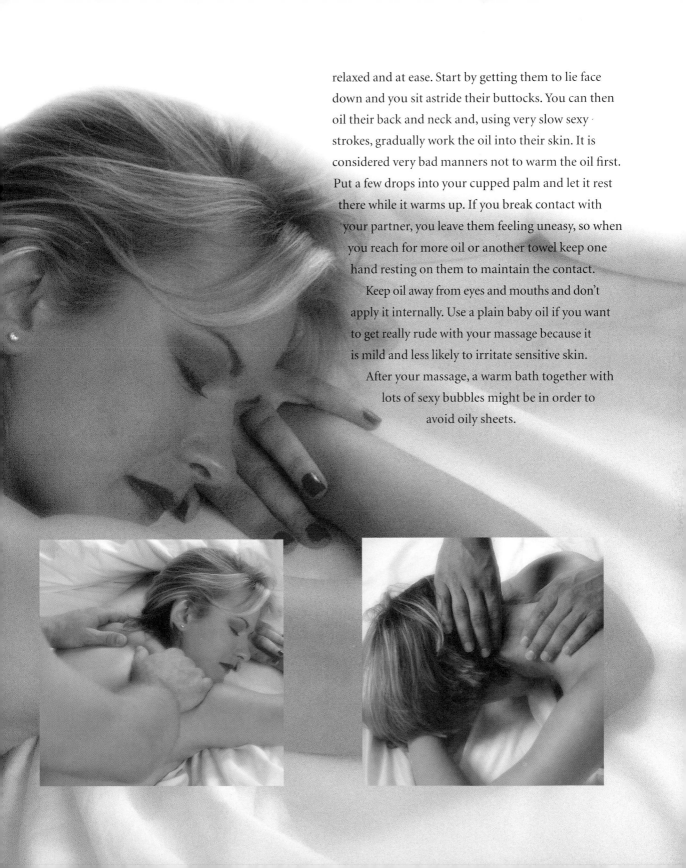

relaxed and at ease. Start by getting them to lie face down and you sit astride their buttocks. You can then oil their back and neck and, using very slow sexy strokes, gradually work the oil into their skin. It is considered very bad manners not to warm the oil first. Put a few drops into your cupped palm and let it rest there while it warms up. If you break contact with your partner, you leave them feeling uneasy, so when you reach for more oil or another towel keep one hand resting on them to maintain the contact.

Keep oil away from eyes and mouths and don't apply it internally. Use a plain baby oil if you want to get really rude with your massage because it is mild and less likely to irritate sensitive skin.

After your massage, a warm bath together with lots of sexy bubbles might be in order to avoid oily sheets.

Foreplay is all the things you do before having sex to get the juices going and to build up the excitement—but where do we draw the line between foreplay and loveplay?

Foreplay

IDEALLY, FOREPLAY SHOULD be going on all the time, even while just holding hands. But in this section we will look at some techniques you can use just prior to lovemaking and in the next section we will look at loveplay.

Everyone does foreplay—even kissing is foreplay. A certain level of foreplay is always necessary and probably already indulged in. What we are looking for here are new and interesting ideas for increasing sexual excitement—and especially the seductive techniques.

Do you spend enough time kissing? This is something that can be extremely erotic if really indulged in. Don't neglect tongue sucking, which is very erotic, and also making your kisses as wet as possible; dry kisses are not very sexy. Practice lip sucking—taking your partner's top or bottom lip into your mouth and sucking hard on it.

As well as "French" kissing (open mouths and with tongues) you can kiss your lover's body all over. The way to do this is to French kiss any bits you want with

lots of wetness and lots of tongue. A man can not only perform oral sex on his lover but also kiss her clitoris, taking it into his mouth and sucking hard on it and tonguing it vigorously as if he were kissing her mouth. His tongue can be pushed into her vagina and the same kissing techniques used (but never ever blow, for this can be dangerous). For the woman, kissing the man's penis should be done wetly, moistly, with her whole mouth and tongue. She can run her open mouth up and down the shaft and let her teeth gently rub against it. The area behind the penis where it joins the scrotum shouldn't be neglected because this is especially sensitive. And for both men and women the perineum (that tiny bit of very sensitive skin joining the genitals to the anus) shouldn't be ignored as an erotic area to be kissed, licked, sucked, and stimulated with fingers. If any tongue to anus contact is indulged in, avoid subsequent tongue to genitals so that no infection can be transferred— the same goes for fingers.

Obviously, when you are kissing your lover's body all over, you will also be using your hands and fingers to stimulate them. Dry skin-to-skin contact is not as sexy as wetness. The nerve endings seem to respond better—maybe it's a better conductivity of electrical impulses—if the skin is moist in some way. Saliva is obviously on hand, so to speak, and works well but don't neglect lotions and potions. This is why massage oils are so effective, because they improve the skin-to-skin contact. There should be no taboo areas on your lover's body where you can't, or shouldn't, touch but they may have their own view about this, so learn from them. The man can stimulate his partner's breasts and nipples but the woman shouldn't overlook the man's nipples as a very sensitive area for stimulation. Most men's nipples will respond extremely well to be sucked and licked just as will a woman's, and there is something terribly erotic about a woman licking her fingers until they are quite wet and then rubbing them hard across her lover's chest and nipples.

Real sexual excitement is a question of not what you do but when you do it. If the man is licking his partner's clitoris and inserts a finger or two into her vagina he needs to be sure her vulva is wet enough and aroused enough before he does it. He can also, if he is adept enough and doesn't mind a little hand cramp, lick her clitoris and insert a finger into her vagina and his thumb gently into her rectum (again with moistness); this leaves his other hand free to caress her breasts or push his fingers into her mouth so she can suck on them as she comes.

The woman can suck her lover's penis and push one finger into his rectum and use her thumb to stimulate his perineum; this leaves her other hand free to massage his penis, push fingers into his mouth, stimulate his nipples, or whatever he prefers.

Most people who have had a one-night stand report that although the sex might have been great it still left them with a feeling of something missing. That something may well be love. If you're not in love, you cannot hope to make sexual contact with your partner on a very deep level.

Loveplay

Really good sex and seduction techniques have a lot to do with trust, respect, care, and understanding. If you are isolated as a couple and speak a different emotional language then your contact in bed will go astray. If you laugh a lot together; share a lot of time together talking and responding; if you both genuinely like each other, then good sexual relations are easily improved.

Loveplay is about touching each other without it necessarily being sexual touching. Holding hands is loveplay; oral sex is foreplay. Yet without holding hands a lot, the oral sex is either going to stop, or, if it does happen, it will be unsatisfactory because the lover's heart isn't in it.

Loveplay starts with waking up in the morning. If you wake up grumpy and just get out of bed then your lover will start their day feeling rejected before their day has even started. How can you expect them to make passionate love to you later? Wake up first and then reach over and kiss your lover, stroke their hair, ask them how they slept, make the coffee or tea, run

them a bath, pamper them, flatter them, tell them you love them (this one especially and a lot). If you do all this, you've made them feel special, excited, cared about before they have even got out of bed. What a glorious start to their day. Then, if later on, you make love they'll already be halfway to passion.

Once you're both up don't let the loveplay stop. Touch them constantly, stroke their hand, kiss them, hold hands when you're out together, put your arm around their waist, hug them, keep telling them you love them, hug them some more, offer to help in whatever way they want you to. None of this makes you a doormat, they are just the first steps to making you the best lover in the world.

Loveplay is about having fun together in a physical way and not necessarily about having sex. You can fondle and stroke, be sexy and provocative, tease and flirt, be naughty and rude, whatever you feel as long as you are being both respectful and tantalizing. Allow your lover lots of space as well as being very close. If they are concentrating on something, they may not appreciate your fondling their buttocks or tweaking their nipples. If they are doing the dishes at the sink they may respond well, however, to having the back of their neck rubbed, kissed, sucked, and licked.

The best combination for loveplay is to be both courteous and naughty. Offer to go shopping with them and then see how often you can touch them intimately without getting caught.

When you are out in a car together the passenger can rest one hand lightly on the driver's thigh. This isn't distracting since it isn't foreplay or sexual but it is reassuring, tender, and somehow erotic. It makes you both stay in touch. You can do the same watching television or visiting the theater; if it's dark and safe enough you can fool around some more and make it sexual. What you have to avoid is the absence of touch, the isolation, the not being friends, the touching only when one of you wants sex. If the touching is going on all the time then the transition to sex is very easy—not too much of a shock or change of pace or direction. If the touching only happens for sexual reasons, it can seem abrupt and disrespectful.

Loveplay is what you do before foreplay and, as such, is just as much fun. You can be as silly and as close as you want to be—have pillow fights, run around the house naked, tickle each other, have wrestling matches in the nude, have custard pie fights (in the nude of course), wrap each other in plastic wrap, go for long walks dressed only in long winter coats (stark naked underneath is essential), smear jelly over each other, expose yourselves to each other in tantalizing flashes of naughtiness when the other is on the phone, phone each other up at work and make the most outrageously sexy suggestions for lovemaking later on, be dressed in your sexiest clothes when your partner comes home and reveal bits of yourself very slowly over the course of the evening, bath together and soap some bits more than others.

120

Loveplay is about setting up sexual tension—without resolving it. You could go on a picnic together and enjoy the food, the sunshine, and the countryside. You then have a choice—fool around a little and save the lovemaking until later, or go for it then and there. The trouble is, there may be people around, or the location is full of wasps or ants, or the sun is likely to go in at any moment and it's going to rain. If you save the lovemaking until later and just indulge in a little loveplay you won't suffer the disappointment you would if you were about to come and somebody walked past with their dog. Loveplay is all about increasing that excitement—but delaying the orgasm until later when the location or circumstances may be better. It's the appetizer without the main course—which isn't being denied, merely saved with anticipation.

The other important thing with loveplay is to make sure it continues during sex. You don't have to go all serious just because you're making love—keep the jokes going and the laughter. You can still tickle each other or flick noses or whatever it is that you normally do. Loveplay means that sex can be more fun and you can be your

real self. Some lovers seem to change personality during sex—which can be extremely disconcerting for their partner. They go all serious and grownup as if sex was a task or a terribly difficult job to do—it isn't; it's the easiest thing in the world if you approach it the right way.

If your normal lovemaking lasts only a few minutes and is infrequent, you might try looking to your loveplay first rather than to your sexual techniques. If you aren't having fun with your lover during your normal

daytime routine then how can you possibly expect to have fun making love later on? If you and your lover aren't really good friends and in love as well as loving each other then you can't really expect your partner to be as open and as sexually adventurous as you would like.

Talking to your lover is all part of loveplay—making them feel special and important.

Some people treat their lover worse than they would treat a stranger. If you are intolerant or judgmental of them, they won't respond as well to you sexually as they would if you were praising and supportive. Treat your lover as your equal—you did this when you first met them, and it is only time and familiarity that makes us indifferent or unsympathetic to a partner. If you really want your sexual excitement to be wanton, interesting, and rewarding, then you have to put in some work beforehand and that is an investment well worth making.

Tantric Lovemaking

Tantra means text—and tantric sex means sacred sex as laid out in very early sex manuals written by the Hindus. Sacred sex is sex as a tool to meditation, enlightenment, and spiritual advancement. However, it can still be fun and useful as a means of raising sexual excitement.

THE TANTRIC TEXTS contain explicit and very detailed instructions on how to make love. Some of the sexual instruction, though amusing, is very difficult unless you are double-jointed or a contortionist. They are only for very advanced practitioners of tantra. However, there are other bits you can try in order to make your sex life zing a little. Try some of the following for some fun.

THE CONGRESS OF THE COW

The woman stands upright and bends forward until her hands touch the ground. The man then enters her from behind and clasps her around the waist much as a bull would mount a cow. In this position he can also stimulate her clitoris, and his pelvic bone will be able to stimulate the area around her buttocks and perineum.

THE CONGRESS OF THE ELEPHANT

The woman lies face down and the man enters her from behind with his legs outside hers. He should support his weight on his arms. The woman, by pressing her thighs tightly together, should be able to provide extra friction for the man if required.

THE CONGRESS OF THE VINE

The couple have sex standing up with the man leaning back against a wall for support. The woman should entwine her legs around the back of the man's thighs. It's probably best if she tries this with only one leg at a time unless he is very strong and she is very athletic. If the couple are of very different heights the man should bend his knees and keep his legs apart so that he can lower himself to the woman's level.

THE CONGRESS OF THE MONKEY

The man leans back against a wall for support and the woman clasps him around the neck. If he bends his knees, she will be able to grip the back of his thighs with her heels and use her toes against the wall for extra thrust. The man should grip the woman around the upper thighs and help to support her like that. Both this position and the preceding one are good for spontaneous sex and indulging in erotic kissing.

THE PAIR OF TONGS

The man lies down and the woman sits astride him, facing him, with her knees bent back. There need be no thrusting if the woman has tight vagina muscles; she can just gently squeeze his penis. The man, in this position, can caress the woman's breasts and she can stimulate her own clitoris—or the man can.

THE SPINNING TOP

The couple begin as the Pair of Tongs but the woman slowly, and carefully, swivels around until she is facing away from the man.

THE SWING

The man sits half upright and the woman sits in his lap facing away from him. She should support her weight by gripping his ankles and the man should support his own weight by propping himself up on his arms. In this position the woman can, as the name suggests, swing herself backward and forwards, or even from side to side.

THE CONGRESS OF THE MARE

The woman sits as for the Swing, in the man's lap while he is sitting half upright. Instead of leaning forward, she can lean back. The man should take his weight on his arms. This should leave the woman free to stimulate her clitoris and the man can kiss her neck and shoulders. If the woman does lean forward, she can grip her partner's ankles and can then exert considerable pressure and friction on his penis while still maintaining control.

Index

Acknowledgments

The author would like to thank Debbie Thorpe and Donna Wood for their support and enthusiasm and all the people at Bridgewater Books who have provided such fascinating and original design work and Peter Pugh-Cook for his photography. He would also like to thank Roni Jay for her help with some of the practical exercises in this book, which needed trying out—a lot!